The Holman

CONCISE
BIBLE
ATLAS

The Holman

CONCISE BIBLE ATLAS

Holman Bible Publishers
Nashville

Library of Congress Card Number: 82-80103

Printed in Israel

CONTENTS

CHRONOLOGICAL TABLE

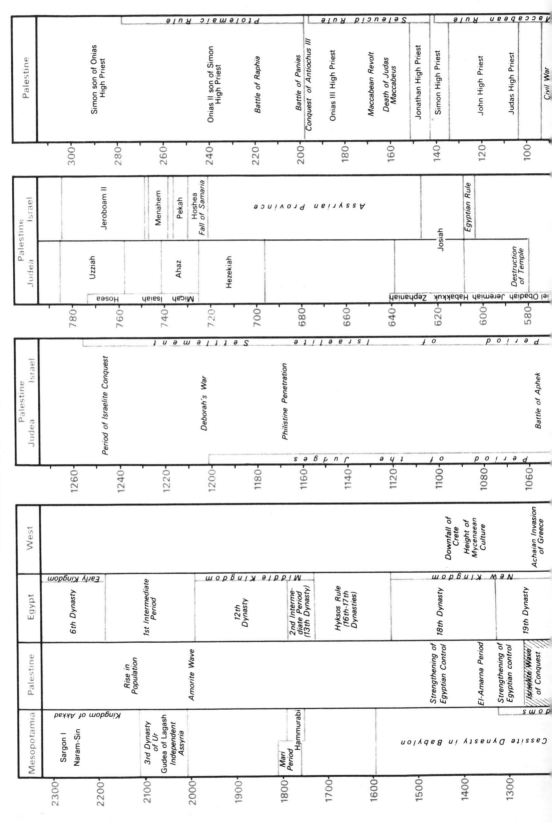

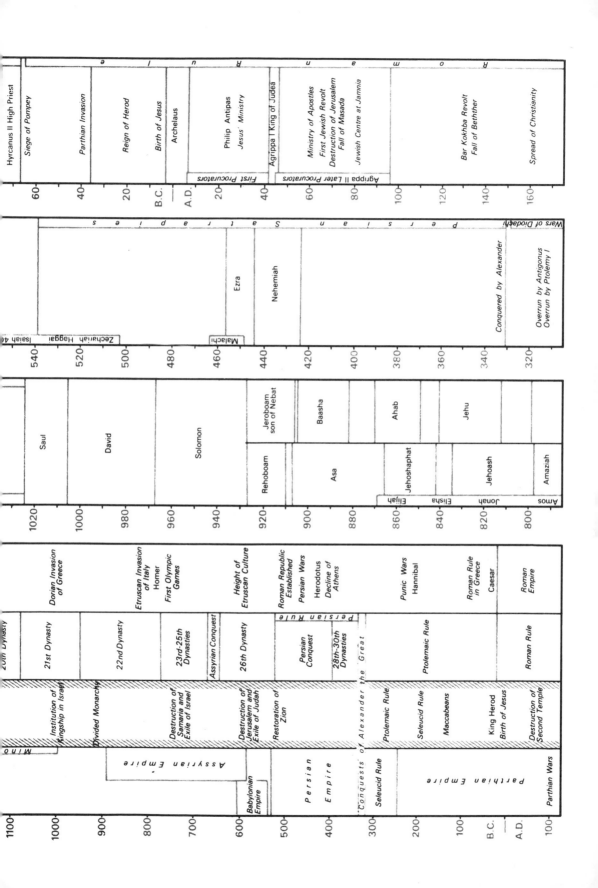

TO THE READER

This Atlas has been specially designed to help you
understand and enjoy the Bible. Although it is
concise and easy to follow you will discover that
it is packed with information. An index with
almost 900 entries makes all this material instantly
available.

The maps and city plans tell you about places and
frontiers and distances at every period of Bible
history. The illustrations provide fascinating
archaeological and cultural data. A time chart
relates the different strands of Bible history to
what was going on elsewhere in the ancient world.

From the Atlas you can learn about the commerce of
the ancient Near East, the wanderings of ancient
peoples, the major travel routes and the rise of
Christianity. It has been researched and produced by
specialists to bring a new dimension to your study
of the Bible

The Publishers

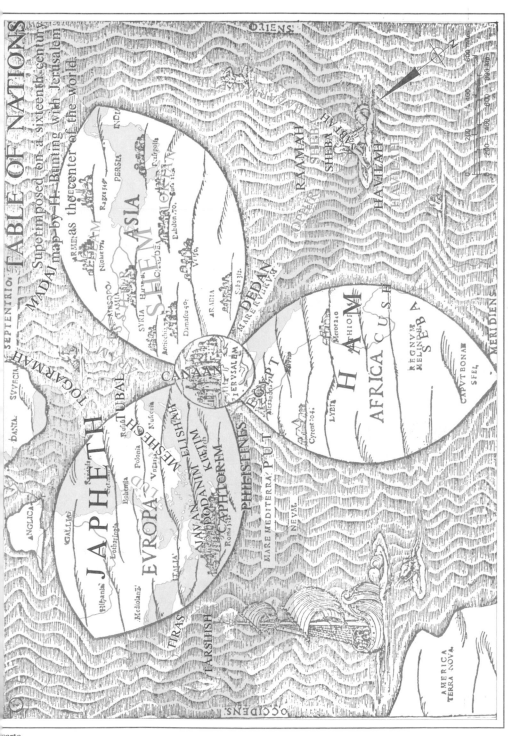

TABLE OF NATIONS

Superimposed on a sixteenth-century map by H. Bunting, with Jerusalem as the center of the world.

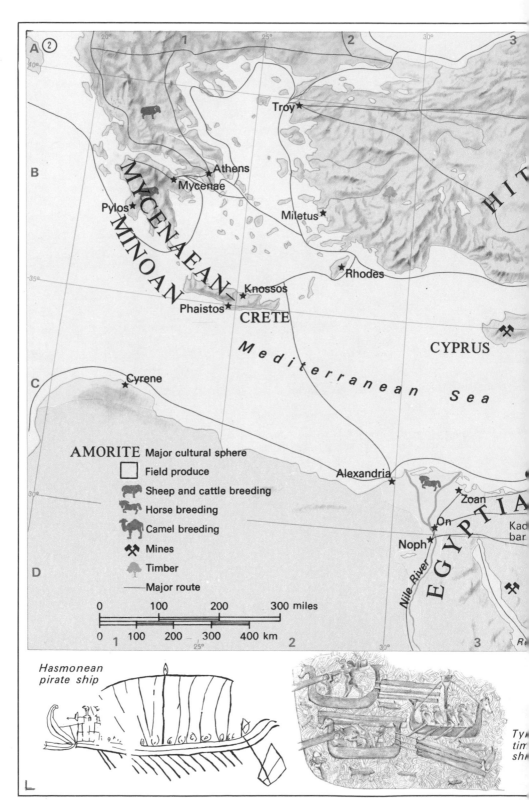

A ② 20° 1 25° 2 30° 3

Troy★

B

MYCENAEAN

Athens★
Mycenae★

Pylos★

MINOAN

Miletus★

35°

Rhodes★

Knossos★
Phaistos★

CRETE

CYPRUS

M e d i t e r r a n e a n   S e a

C

Cyrene★

AMORITE Major cultural sphere

☐ Field produce

🐏 Sheep and cattle breeding

🐎 Horse breeding

🐫 Camel breeding

⚒ Mines

🌲 Timber

— Major route

Alexandria★

Zoan★

On★

Noph★

EGYPTIA

Kad
bar

30°

HIT

HI

D

| 0 | 100 | 200 | 300 miles |

| 0 | 100 | 200 | 300 | 400 km |

1 25° 2 30° 3 R

Nile River

*Hasmonean
pirate ship*

*Ty
tim
sh*

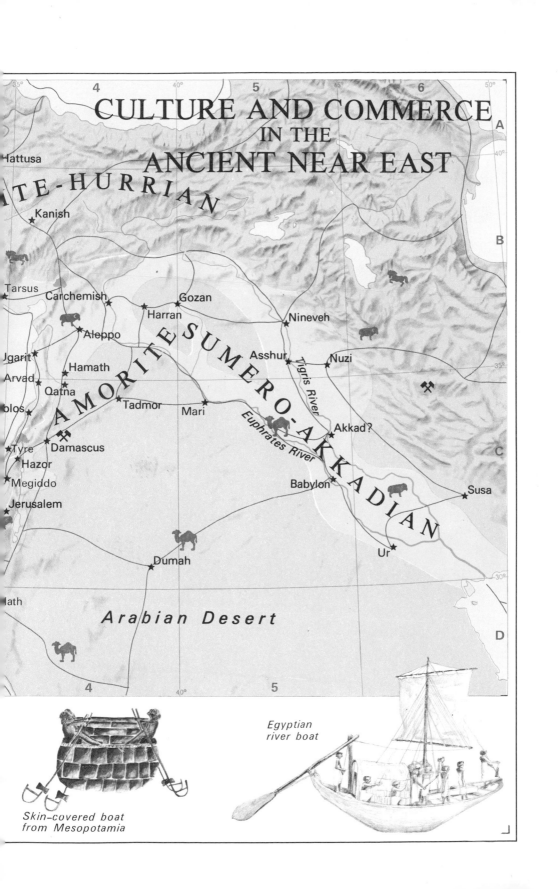

CULTURE AND COMMERCE
IN THE
ANCIENT NEAR EAST

Hattusa

TE-HURRIAN

Kanish

Tarsus

Carchemish

Harran

Gozan

Nineveh

Aleppo

Ugarit

Hamath

Asshur

Nuzi

Arvad

Qatna

Tadmor

Mari

Tigris River

Akkad?

blos

AMORITE

SUMERO-AKKADIAN

Tyre

Damascus

Euphrates River

Hazor

Megiddo

Babylon

Susa

Jerusalem

Ur

Dumah

Arabian Desert

Math

Egyptian
river boat

Skin–covered boat
from Mesopotamia

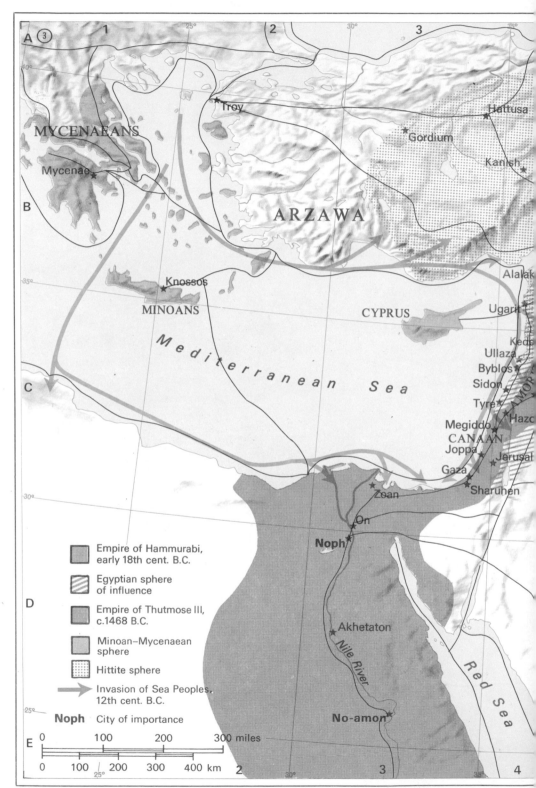

A ③ 1 25° 2 30° 3 35°

40°

★ Troy

★ Hattusa

MYCENAEANS

★ Gordium

★ Mycenae

Kanish ★

B

ARZAWA

Alalak

35°

★ Knossos

Ugarit ★

MINOANS

CYPRUS

Kedi

Ullaza ★

Byblos ★

Sidon ★

C

M e d i t e r r a n e a n   S e a

Tyre ★

Hazo

Megiddo ★

CANAAN

Joppa ★

Jerusal

Gaza ★

Sharuhen ★

30°

★ Zoan

★ On

Noph ★

	Empire of Hammurabi, early 18th cent. B.C.
	Egyptian sphere of influence
	Empire of Thutmose III, c.1468 B.C.
	Minoan–Mycenaean sphere
	Hittite sphere
→	Invasion of Sea Peoples, 12th cent. B.C.

Noph City of importance

D

★ Akhetaton

Nile River

Red Sea

25°

E   0   100   200   300 miles

0   100   200   300   400 km

25° 2   30° 3   35° 4

No-amon ★

© carta

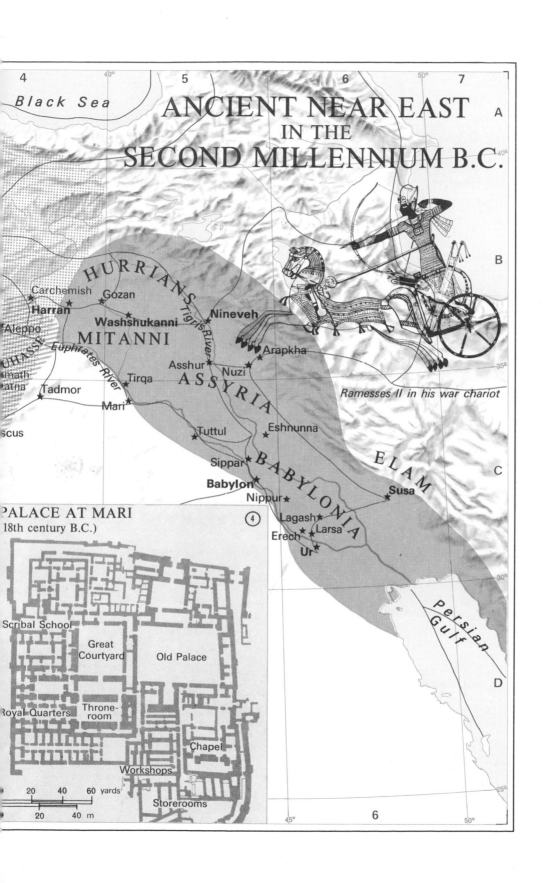

4　　40° 5　　6　　50° 7

Black Sea

ANCIENT NEAR EAST
IN THE
SECOND MILLENNIUM B.C.

A

B

HURRIANS

Carchemish　Gozan
Harran
Aleppo
Washshukanni
MITANNI
Nineveh
Arapkha
Asshur
Nuzi
Tirqa
ASSYRIA

Tadmor
Mari

scus

Tuttul

Eshnunna

ELAM

Sippar
BABYLONIA
Babylon
Nippur
Susa

C

Ramesses II in his war chariot

Lagash
Larsa
Erech
Ur

PALACE AT MARI
(18th century B.C.)

④

Scribal School

Great
Courtyard

Old Palace

Royal Quarters

Throne-
room

Chapel

Workshops

20　40　60 yards

20　　40 m

Storerooms

Persian Gulf

D

45°　　6　　50°

35°

30°

25°

40°

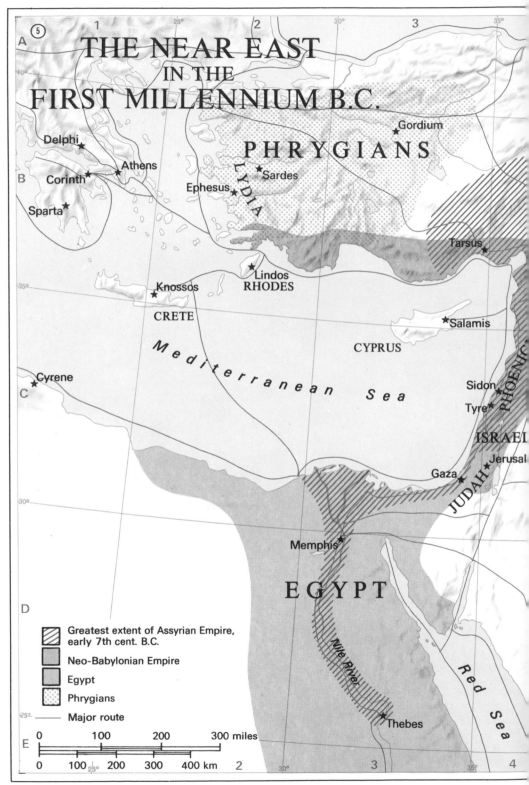

THE NEAR EAST
IN THE
FIRST MILLENNIUM B.C.

★ Gordium

P H R Y G I A N S

Delphi ★

★ Athens
Corinth ★
LYDIA ★ Sardes
Sparta ★
Ephesus ★

★ Tarsus

★ Lindos
Knossos ★ RHODES

CRETE
★ Salamis

Cyrene ★
CYPRUS

M e d i t e r r a n e a n   S e a

Sidon ★
Tyre ★ PHOENIC.

ISRAEL
Jerusal ★
Gaza ★ JUDAH

Memphis ★

EGYPT

Nile River

Red Sea

	Greatest extent of Assyrian Empire, early 7th cent. B.C.
	Neo-Babylonian Empire
	Egypt
	Phrygians
—	Major route

★ Thebes

| 0 | 100 | 200 | 300 miles |
| 0 | 100 200 | 300 | 400 km |

© carta

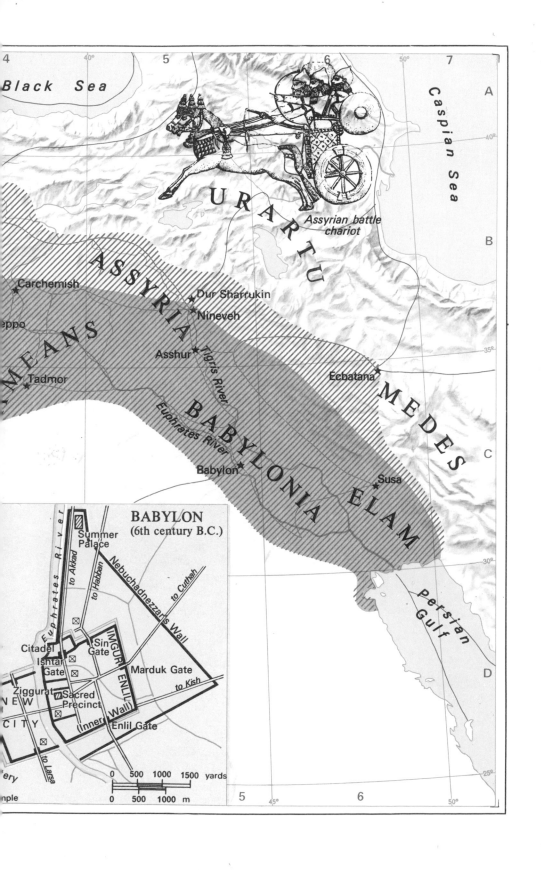

Black Sea

Caspian Sea

URARTU

Assyrian battle chariot

ASSYRIA

Carchemish

Dur Sharrukin

Nineveh

eppo

MEANS

Asshur

Tigris River

Tadmor

Ecbatana

MEDES

Euphrates River

BABYLONIA

Babylon

ELAM

Susa

Persian Gulf

BABYLON
(6th century B.C.)

Euphrates River

Summer Palace

to Akkad

to Habban

Nebuchadnezzar's Wall

to Cutah

Citadel

Sin Gate

IMGUR ENLIL

Ishtar Gate

Marduk Gate

to Kish

Ziggurat

Sacred Precinct

NEW

(Inner Wall)

CITY

Enlil Gate

to Larsa

ery

temple

| 0 | 500 | 1000 | 1500 | yards |

| 0 | 500 | 1000 | m |

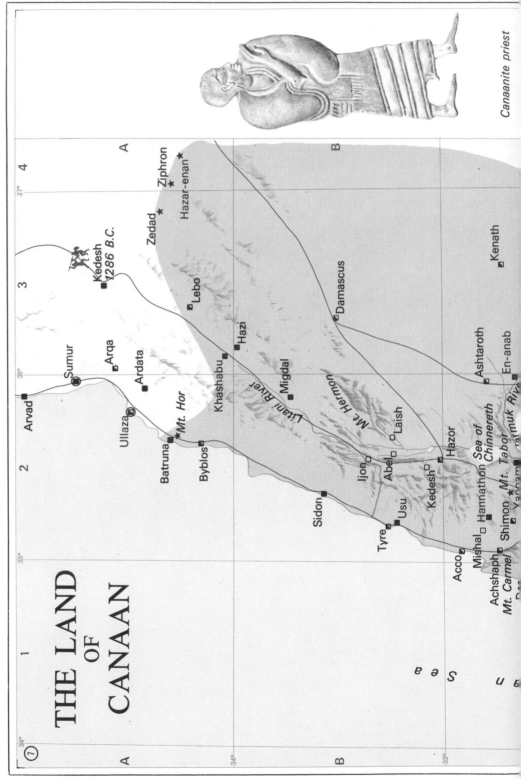

THE LAND OF CANAAN

Canaanite priest

© carta

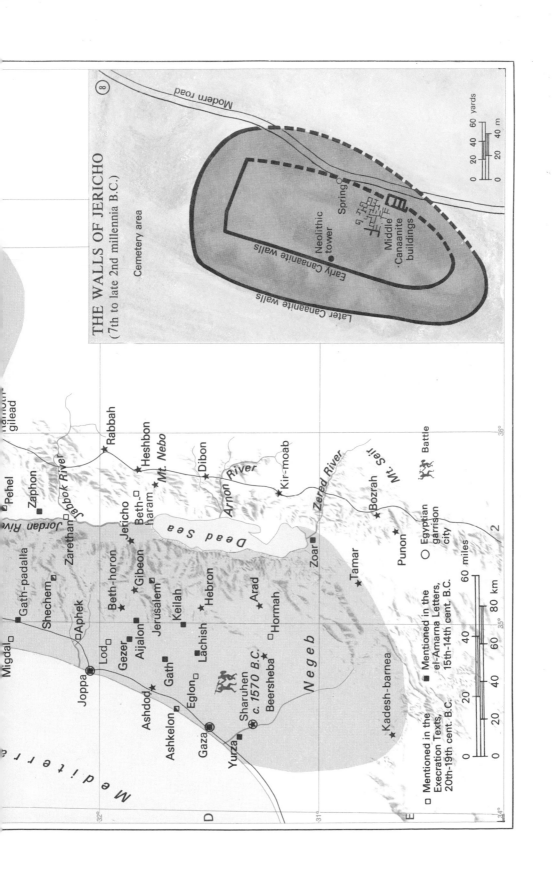

THE WALLS OF JERICHO
(7th to late 2nd millennia B.C.)

Cemetery area

Later Canaanite walls

Early Canaanite walls

Neolithic tower

Spring

Middle Canaanite buildings

Modern road

8

0   20   40   60 yards

0   20   40 m

Migdal

Mediterranea

Joppa

Lod

Ashdod

Gezer

Aphek

Shechem

Gath-padalla

Pehel

Zaphon

Zarethan

Jericho

Beth-horon

Gibeon

Jerusalem

Aijalon

Gath

Keilah

Lachish

Hebron

Ashkelon

Eglon

Gaza

Yurza

Sharuhen
c. 1570 B.C.

Beersheba

Hormah

Arad

Negeb

Kadesh-barnea

Dead Sea

Jordan River

Jabbok River

Rabbah

Heshbon

Beth-haram

Mt. Nebo

Dibon

Arnon River

Kir-moab

Zered River

Bozrah

Mt. Seir

Zoar

Tamar

Punon

Battle

Egyptian garrison city

gilead

□ Mentioned in the
  Execration Texts,
  20th-19th cent. B.C.

■ Mentioned in the
  el-Amarna Letters,
  15th-14th cent. B.C.

0   20   40   60 miles

0   20   40   60   80 km

32°

31°

34°

35°

36°

2

D

E

THE COMING
OF THE
ISRAELITES

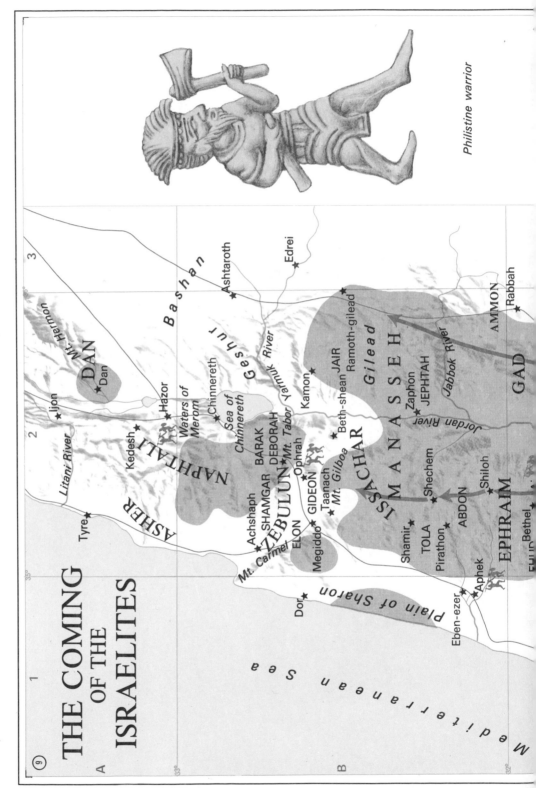

Philistine warrior

© carta

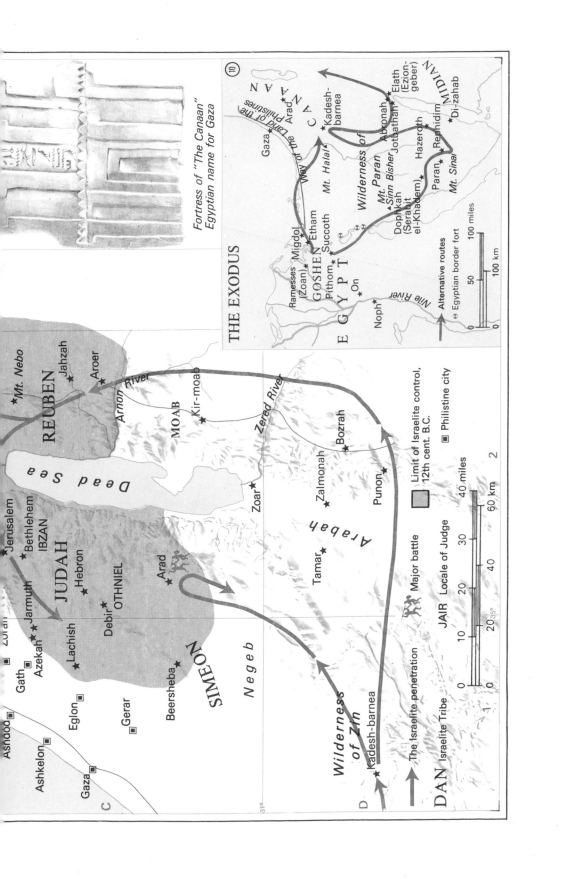

Fortress of "The Canaan"
Egyptian name for Gaza

THE EXODUS

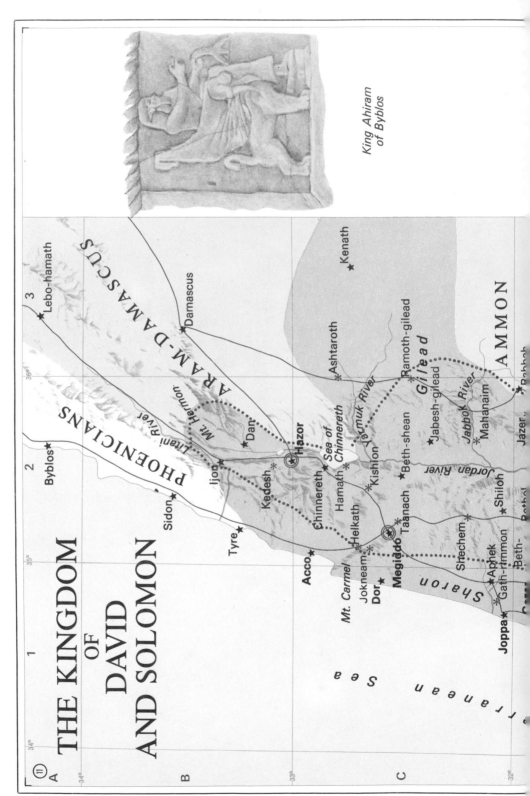

THE KINGDOM
OF
DAVID
AND SOLOMON

King Ahiram
of Byblos

PHOENICIANS

ARAM-DAMASCUS

Lebo-hamath

Byblos

Sidon

Tyre

Acco

Mt. Carmel

Dor

Jokneam

Megiddo

Joppa

Sharon

Litani River

Mt. Hermon

Ijon

Kedesh

Hazor

Dan

Damascus

Ashtaroth

Kenath

Chinnereth

Sea of
Chinnereth

Hamath

Helkath

Taanach

Shechem

Aphek

Gath-rimmon

Beth-

Beth-

Bethel

Shiloh

Kishon

Yarmuk River

Beth-shean

Jabesh-gilead

Jordan River

Mahanaim

Jabbok River

Jazer

Ramoth-gilead

Gilead

AMMON

Rabbah

Mediterranean Sea

© carta

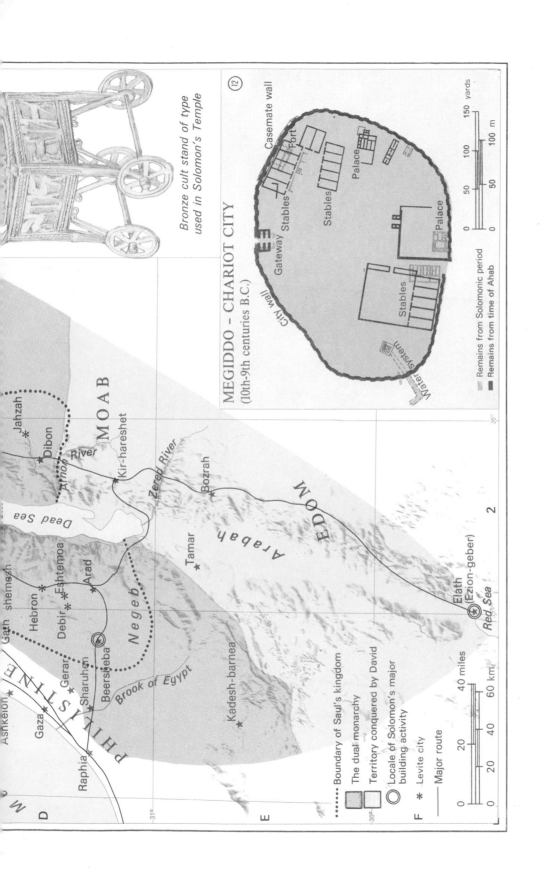

Bronze cult stand of type
used in Solomon's Temple

MEGIDDO – CHARIOT CITY
(10th-9th centuries B.C.)

Casemate wall

Fort

Gateway Stables

Stables

Palace

Stables

Palace

City wall

Water
system

⑫

150 yards

100 m

50

50

0

0

50

0

░░ Remains from Solomonic period

■ Remains from time of Ahab

PHILISTINE

MOAB

Ashkelon

Jahzah

Gaza

Dibon

Arnon River

Raphia

Gerar

Gath shemesh

Hebron

Eshtemoa

Debir

Arad

Kir-hareshet

Sharuhen

Beersheba

Dead Sea

Zered River

Bozrah

Negeb

Tamar

Arabah

EDOM

Brook of Egypt

Kadesh-barnea

Elath
(Ezion-geber)

Red Sea

········ Boundary of Saul's kingdom

The dual monarchy

Territory conquered by David

⊚ Locale of Solomon's major
  building activity

✱ Levite city

—— Major route

0   20   40 miles

0   20   40   60 km

D

E

F

M o
a

31°

30°

35°

2

36°

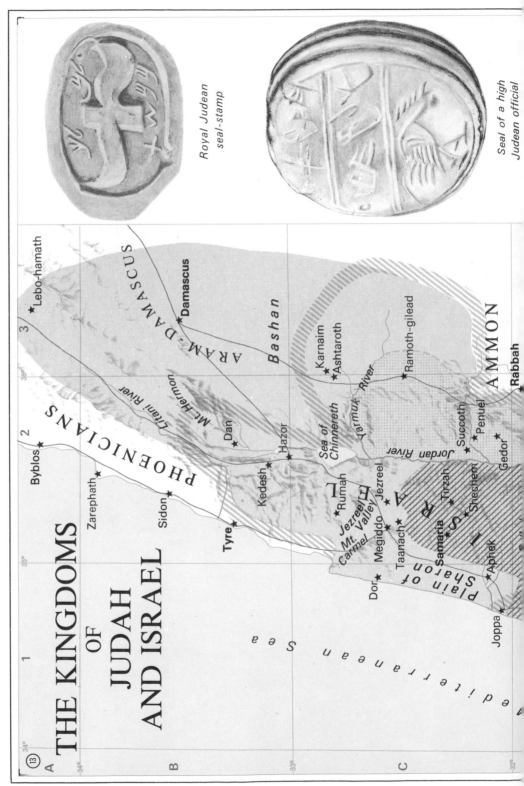

THE KINGDOMS
OF
JUDAH
AND ISRAEL

Royal Judean
seal-stamp

Seal of a high
Judean official

Lebo-hamath

Byblos

Zarephath

Sidon

PHOENICIANS

Tyre

Kedesh

Hazor

Dan

Mt. Hermon

Litani River

ARAM-DAMASCUS

Damascus

Bashan

Karnaim
Ashtaroth

Sea of
Chinnereth

Yarmuk River

Ramoth-gilead

Jordan River

AMMON

Rabbah

Succoth

Penuel

Gedor

Rumah

Jezreel

ISRAEL

Jezreel
Valley

Mt.
Carmel

Megiddo

Taanach

Samaria

Tirzah

Shechem

Dor

Plain of
Sharon

Aphek

Joppa

Mediterranean Sea

© carta

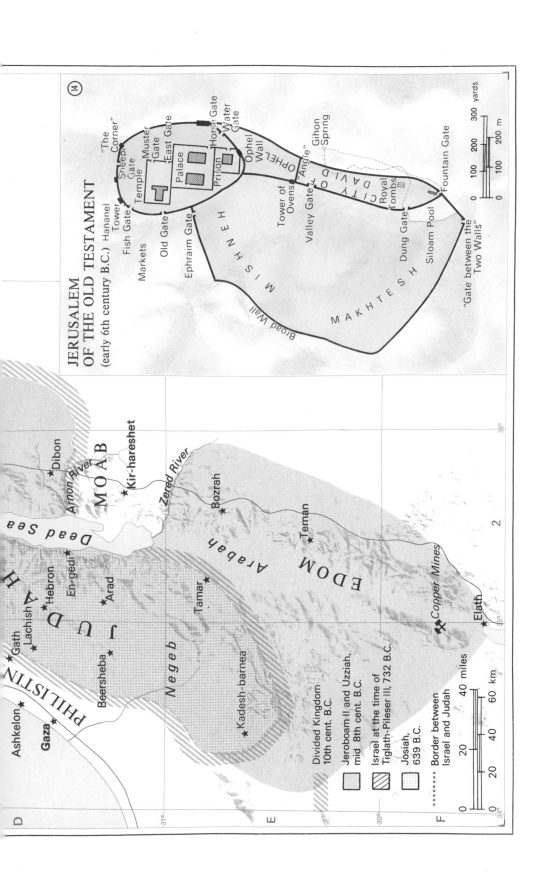

JERUSALEM
OF THE OLD TESTAMENT
(early 6th century B.C.)

⑭

"The Corner"
Hananel Tower
Muster Gate
Sheep Gate
East Gate
Fish Gate
Temple
Horse Gate
Water Gate
Palace
Markets
Old Gate
Prison
Ophel Wall
Ephraim Gate
OPHEL
"Angle"
Gihon Spring
Tower of Ovens
CITY OF DAVID
Royal Tombs
Valley Gate
Dung Gate
M I S H N E H
Siloam Pool
Broad Wall
Fountain Gate
M A K H T E S H
"Gate between the Two Walls"

0   100   200   300 yards
0   100   200 m

Dibon
Arnon River
M O A B
Kir-hareshet
Zered River
Dead Sea
Bozrah
Sea
En-gedi
Hebron
Arad
Teman
Lachish
Gath
Ashkelon
Gaza
PHILISTIN
J U D A H
Beersheba
Negeb
Tamar
Kadesh-barnea
A r a b a h
E D O M
Copper Mines
Elath

Divided Kingdom 10th cent. B.C.

Jeroboam II and Uzziah, mid 8th cent. B.C.

Israel at the time of Tiglath-Pileser III, 732 B.C.

Josiah, 639 B.C.

········· Border between Israel and Judah

0   20   40 miles
0   20   40   60 km

D

E
31°
30°

F
3°
2
35°
36°

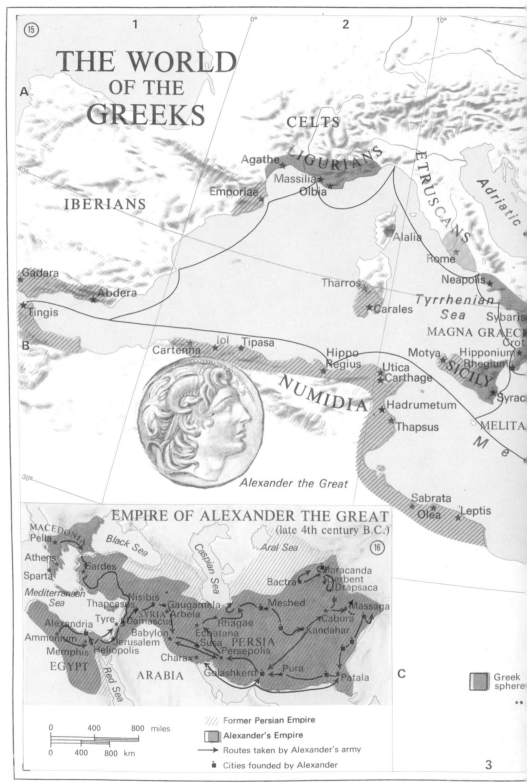

THE WORLD
OF THE
GREEKS

A

CELTS

Agathe

LIGURIANS

Massilia

Emporiae

Olbia

ETRUSCANS

IBERIANS

Adriatic

Alalia

Rome

Gadara

Abdera

Tharros

Neapolis

Tingis

Carales

Tyrrhenian
Sea

Sybaris

MAGNA GRAECIA

Crot

B

Cartenna

Iol Tipasa

Hippo
Regius

Utica

Carthage

Motya

Hipponium

Rhegium

SICILY

Syrac

NUMIDIA

Hadrumetum

Thapsus

MELITA

M
e

Alexander the Great

Sabrata

Olea

Leptis

EMPIRE OF ALEXANDER THE GREAT
(late 4th century B.C.)

MACEDONIA

Pella

Black Sea

Caspian Sea

Aral Sea

⑯

Athens

Sardes

Bactra

Maracanda

Derbent

Drapsaca

Sparta

Mediterranean
Sea

Thapsacus

Nisibis

Gaugamela

Meshed

Massaga

Alexandria

Tyre

SYRIA

Damascus

Arbela

Rhagae

Cabura

Kandahar

Ammonium

Babylon

Ecbatana

Susa

PERSIA

Jerusalem

Memphis

Heliopolis

Charax

Persepolis

EGYPT

Red Sea

ARABIA

Golashkerd

Pura

Patala

C

Greek
sphere

| 0 | 400 | 800 miles |

| 0 | 400 | 800 km |

/// Former Persian Empire

◼ Alexander's Empire

→ Routes taken by Alexander's army

◼ Cities founded by Alexander

3

© carta

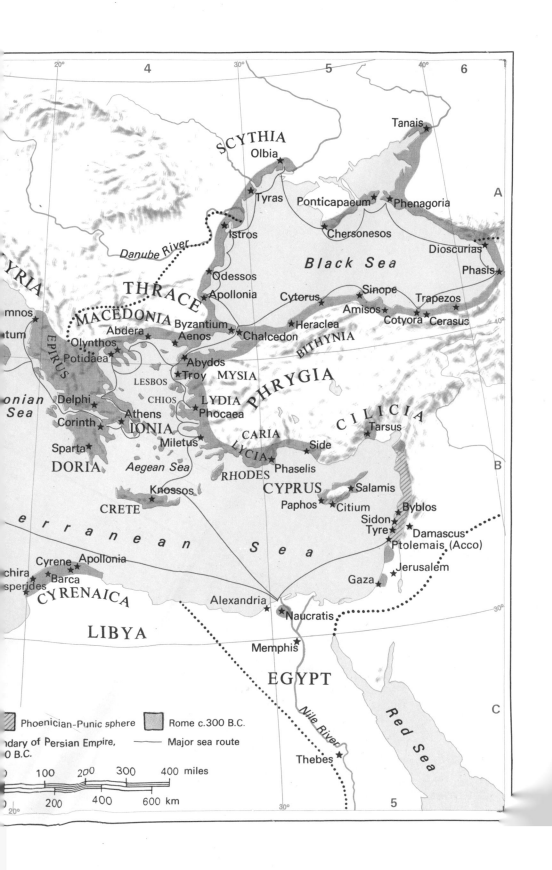

SCYTHIA

Olbia ★

Tyras ★

Ponticapaeum ★ ★ Phenagoria

Tanais ★

Istros ★

Chersonesos ★

Dioscurias ★

Danube River

Odessos ★

Black Sea

Phasis ★

Apollonia ★

Cytorus ★

Sinope ★

Trapezos ★

THRACE

MACEDONIA

Abdera ★

Aenos ★

Byzantium ★ ★ Chalcedon

Heraclea ★

BITHYNIA

Amisos ★

Cotyora ★ Cerasus ★

Olynthos ·

Potidaea ★

EPIRUS

Abydos ★

Troy ★ MYSIA

PHRYGIA

mnos

tum

Ionian Sea

Delphi ★

LESBOS

CHIOS

Corinth ★

Athens ★

IONIA

Sparta ★

Miletus ★

DORIA

Aegean Sea

LYDIA

Phocaea ★

CARIA

LYCIA

Side ★

CILICIA

Tarsus ★

Phaselis ★

Knossos ★

RHODES

CRETE

CYPRUS

Salamis ★

Paphos ★ ★ Citium

Byblos ★

Sidon ★

Tyre ★ ★ Damascus ·

Ptolemais (Acco) ★

Mediterranean Sea

Cyrene ★ Apollonia ★

chira

Barca ★

sperides ·

CYRENAICA

LIBYA

Alexandria ★

★ Naucratis

Jerusalem ★

Gaza ★

Memphis ★

EGYPT

Red Sea

Nile River

Thebes ★

▨ Phoenician-Punic sphere   ▨ Rome c. 300 B.C.

ndary of Persian Empire,   —— Major sea route

0 B.C.

| 100 | 200 | 300 | 400 miles |

| 200 | 400 | 600 km |

⑰

HIBERNIA

BRITANNIA

Eburacum
Lindum
Aquae Sulis
Londinium

North Sea

0°   15°

Atlantic Ocean

45°

GERMANIA

Rhine River

Lutetia

GALLIA

Regina Castra
Vindo

Mediolanum
Burdigala
Lugdunum
Vienna
Genua
Aquileia

RAETIA
NORICUM
PAN

HISPANIA

Nemausus
Narbo
Massilia

ITALIA

ILLYR

Ancona

Toletum
Tarraco

Corduba
Valentia

Rome

Neapolis
Brundisi

Gades

MAURETANIA

Hippo Regius
AFRICA
Carthage

Syracuse

Mediter

ROME (1st-3rd centuries A.D.)

⑱

Castra Praetoria

Circus of Hadrian
Tomb of Augustus
PINCIAN HILL

Circus of Nero
Mausoleum of Hadrian
QUIRINAL HILL
Baths of Diocletian

VATICAN HILL
Pantheon
VIMINAL HILL

Theater of Pompey
Imperial Fora
ESQUILINE HILL

CAPITOLINE HILL
Capitol
Roman Forum
Baths of Trajan

PALATINE HILL
Colosseum

T. Divi Claudii

Circus Maximus
CAELIAN HILL

+ Earliest Christian sites
AVENTINE HILL
Baths of Caracalla

Leptis Magna

C

0   500   1000   1500 yards
0   500   1000 m

2   15°

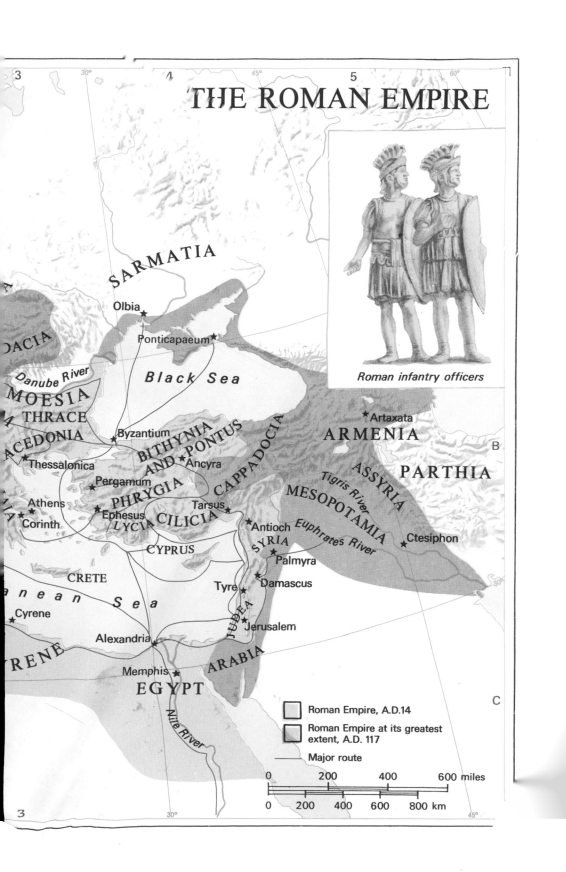

THE ROMAN EMPIRE

Roman infantry officers

SARMATIA

Olbia ★

Ponticapaeum ★

Black Sea

Danube River

DACIA

MOESIA

THRACE

★ Artaxata

ARMENIA

MACEDONIA

Byzantium ★

BITHYNIA AND PONTUS

Ancyra ★

ASSYRIA

PARTHIA

Thessalonica ★

Pergamum ★

CAPPADOCIA

Tigris River

MESOPOTAMIA

Athens ★

PHRYGIA

Tarsus ★

Corinth ★

Ephesus ★

LYCIA

CILICIA

Antioch ★

Euphrates River

Ctesiphon ★

CYPRUS

SYRIA

Palmyra ★

CRETE

Tyre ★

Damascus ★

anean   _Sea_

Cyrene ★

JUDEA

Alexandria ★

Jerusalem ★

YRENE

ARABIA

Memphis ★

EGYPT

Nile River

☐	Roman Empire, A.D.14
☐	Roman Empire at its greatest extent, A.D. 117
—	Major route

0   200   400   600 miles

0   200   400   600   800 km

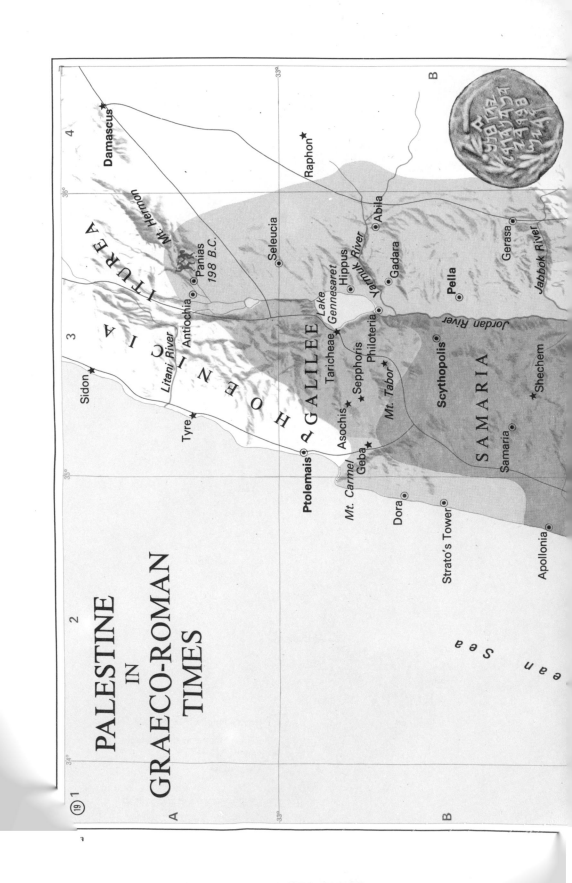

PALESTINE IN GRAECO-ROMAN TIMES

Damascus

Raphon

Mt. Hermon

Seleucia

Panias
198 B.C.

Abila

ITUREA

Gerasa

Jabbok River

Antiochia

Hippus

Gadara

Pella

Litani River

PHOENICIA

Lake
Gennesaret

Yarmuk River

Sidon

GALILEE

Taricheae

Jordan River

Tyre

Asochis

Sepphoris

Philoteria

Scythopolis

Mt. Tabor

Ptolemais

Geba

SAMARIA

Shechem

Mt. Carmel

Samaria

Dora

Strato's Tower

Apollonia

...ean Sea

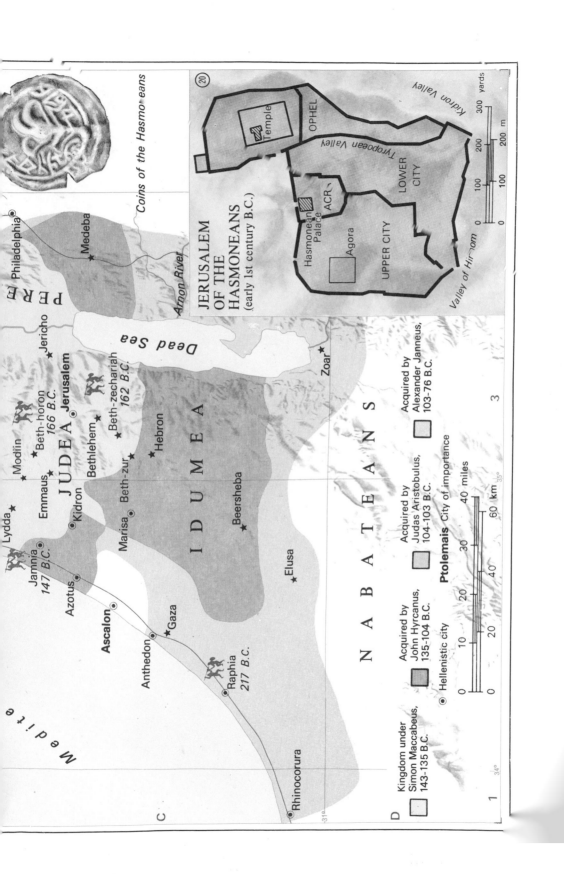

Coins of the Hasmoneans

JERUSALEM OF THE HASMONEANS
(early 1st century B.C.)

Temple

OPHEL

Kidron Valley

Tyropoeon Valley

LOWER CITY

ACRA

Hasmonean Palace

Agora

UPPER CITY

Valley of Hinnom

300 yards

200 m

100

20

Philadelphia

PEREA

Medeba

Arnon River

Dead Sea

Jericho

Beth-horon
166 B.C.

Modiin

Jerusalem

JUDEA

Emmaus

Bethlehem

Beth-zechariah
162 B.C.

Kidron

Lydda

Jamnia
147 B.C.

Azotus

Marisa

Beth-zur

Hebron

IDUMEA

Ascalon

Gaza

Beersheba

Anthedon

Elusa

Raphia
217 B.C.

Zoar

NABATEANS

Rhinocorura

Medite

C

D

Kingdom under
Simon Maccabeus,
143-135 B.C.

Acquired by
John Hyrcanus,
135-104 B.C.

Acquired by
Judas Aristobulus,
104-103 B.C.

Acquired by
Alexander Janneus,
103-76 B.C.

Hellenistic city

Ptolemais City of importance

40 miles

60 km

0 10 20 30

0 20 40

34°

35°

1   2   3

31°

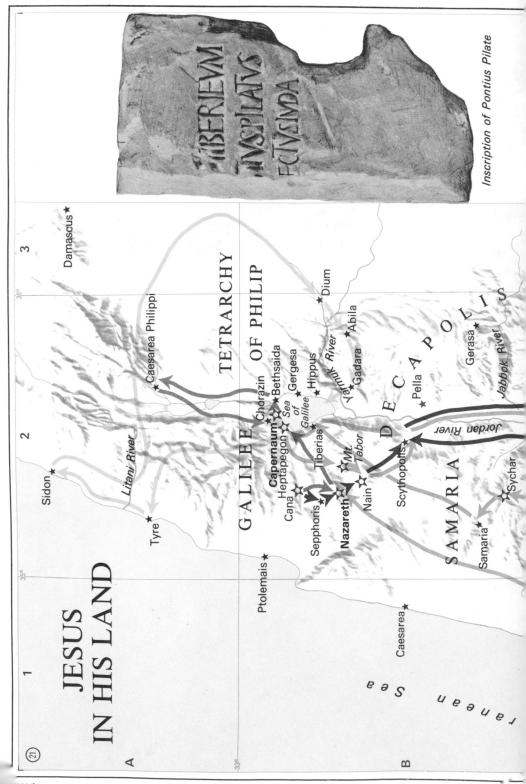

JESUS
IN HIS LAND

Mediterranean Sea

A

B

1   2   3

Ptolemais ★

Sidon ★

Tyre ★

Litani River

Caesarea Philippi ★

Damascus ★

TETRARCHY

OF PHILIP

Chorazin ★

Capernaum ☆
Heptapegon ★

Bethsaida ★

Gergesa ★

Sea of Galilee

Hippus ★

Dium ★

Abila ★

Yarmuk River

Gadara ★

G A L I L E E

Cana ★

Sepphoris ★

Nazareth

Tiberias ★

Mt. Tabor ☆

Nain ★

Scythopolis ☆

D E C A P O L I S

Pella ★

Gerasa ★

Jordan River

Jabbok River

S A M A R I A

Samaria ★

Sychar ☆

Caesarea ★

35°   36°

33°

㉑

carta

Inscription of Pontius Pilate

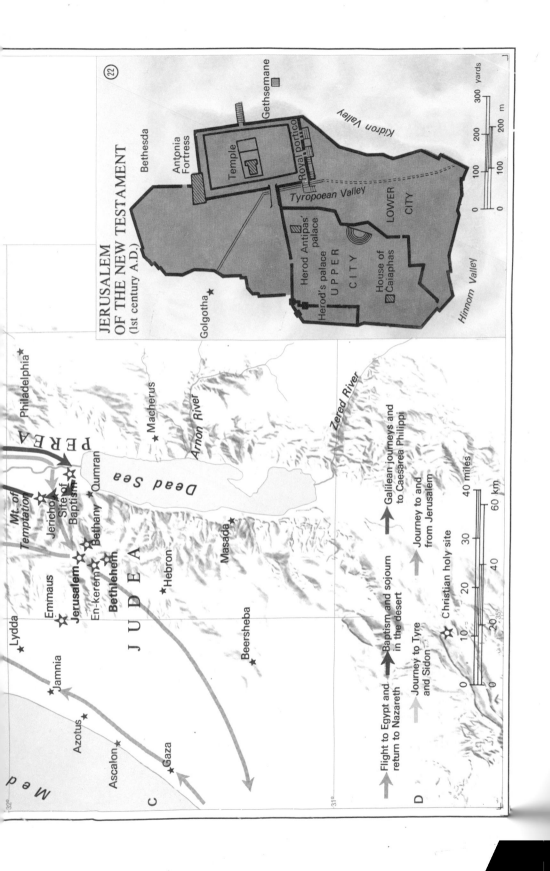

JERUSALEM
OF THE NEW TESTAMENT
(1st century A.D.)

22

Bethesda

Antonia
Fortress

Temple

Royal portico

Gethsemane

Kidron Valley

Tyropoean Valley

Herod Antipas'
palace

Herod's palace

UPPER
CITY

House of
Caiaphas

LOWER
CITY

Hinnom Valley

Golgotha

0   100   200   300 yards

0   100   200 m

Philadelphia

P E R E A

Mt. of
Temptation

Jericho

Site of
Baptism

Bethany

Qumran

Lydda

Emmaus

Jerusalem

En-kerem

Bethlehem

J U D E A

Hebron

Masada

Macherus

Arnon River

Zered River

Dead Sea

Jamnia

Azotus

Ascalon

Gaza

Beersheba

Med

Flight to Egypt and
return to Nazareth

Baptism and sojourn
in the desert

Galilean journeys and
to Caesarea Philippi

Journey to Tyre
and Sidon

Journey to and
from Jerusalem

Christian holy site

0   10   20   30   40 miles

0   20   40   60 km

C

D

32°

31°

35°

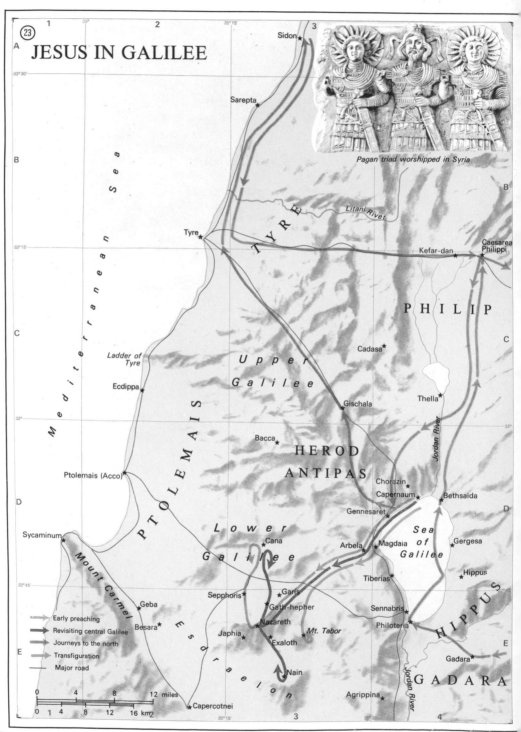

JESUS IN GALILEE

Pagan triad worshipped in Syria

Mediterranean Sea

Sidon

Sarepta

Litani River

TYRE

Tyre

Kefar-dan

Caesarea Philippi

PHILIP

Ladder of Tyre

Upper Galilee

Cadasa

Ecdippa

Gischala

Thella

Jordan River

Bacca

HEROD ANTIPAS

Ptolemais (Acco)

PTOLEMAIS

Chorazin

Capernaum

Bethsaida

Gennesaret

Sycaminum

Lower Galilee

Cana

Arbela

Magdaia

Sea of Galilee

Gergesa

Hippus

Mount Carmel

Tiberias

Geba

Sepphoris

Garis

Gath-hepher

Sennabris

Philoteria

HIPPUS

Besara

Nazareth

Esdraelon

Japhia

Mt. Tabor

Gadara

Exaloth

Nain

Jordan River

GADARA

Agrippina

Capercotnei

Early preaching
Revisiting central Galilee
Journeys to the north
Transfiguration
Major road

0   4   8   12 miles
0 1 4   8   12   16 km

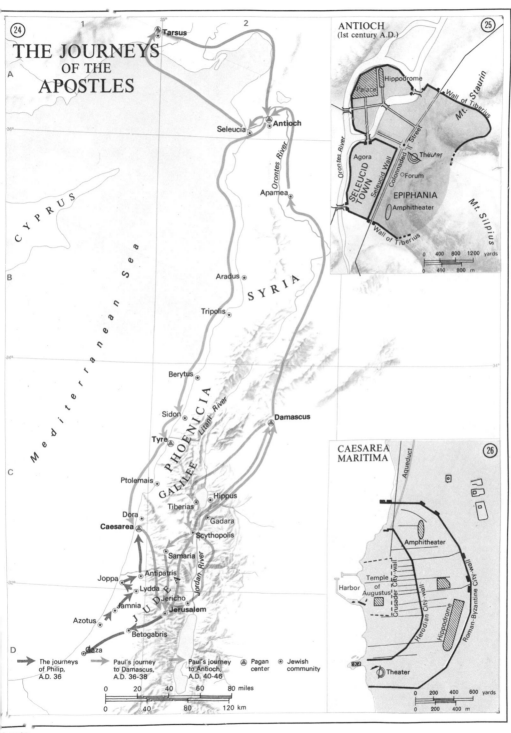

24

THE JOURNEYS
OF THE
APOSTLES

25 ANTIOCH
(1st century A.D.)

Hippodrome

Palace

Wall of Staurin

Mt. Tiberius

Orontes River

Seleucia

Antioch

Agora

Colonnaded Street

Seleucid Wall

Theater

Forum

EPIPHANIA

Amphitheater

Mt. Silpius

Wall of Tiberius

SELEUCID TOWN

Apamea

| 0 | 400 | 800 | 1200 | yards |
| 0 | 400 | 800 | m |

A

Tarsus

1

35°

2

36°

C Y P R U S

M e d i t e r r a n e a n   S e a

Aradus

S Y R I A

Tripolis

34°

34°

Berytus

Litani River

Sidon

P H O E N I C I A

Damascus

Tyre

CAESAREA
MARITIMA

26

Ptolemais

G A L I L E E

Hippus

Aqueduct

Tiberias

Dora

Gadara

Amphitheater

Caesarea

Scythopolis

Temple
of
Augustus

Crusader City-wall

Harbor

Herodian City-wall

Roman-Byzantine City-wall

Hippodrome

Samaria

Jordan River

Joppa

Antipatris

J U D E A

Lydda

Jericho

Jamnia

Jerusalem

Azotus

Betogabris

Theater

Gaza

| 0 | 200 | 400 | 600 | yards |
| 0 | 200 | 400 | m |

D

The journeys
of Philip,
A.D. 36

Paul's journey
to Damascus,
A.D. 36-38

Paul's journey
to Antioch,
A.D. 40-46

Pagan
center

Jewish
community

| 0 | 20 | 40 | 60 | 80 miles |
| 0 | 40 | 80 | 120 km |

32°

© carta

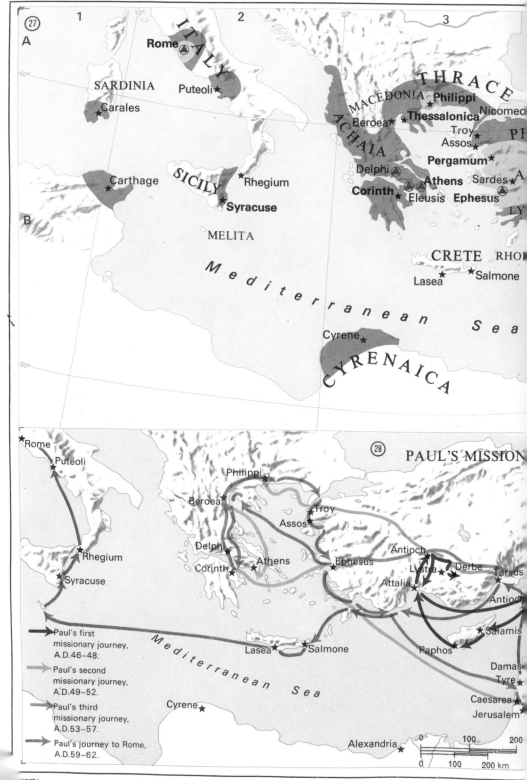

Map 27

A

Rome • ITALY

SARDINIA

Puteoli ★

★ Carales

MACEDONIA ★ **Philippi**

THRACE

★ Beroea ★ **Thessalonica** Nicomed

ACHAIA

Troy ★

Assos ★

Pergamum ★

Carthage ★

SICILY

★ Rhegium

Delphi ▲

★ Syracuse

Athens Sardes ★ A

Eleusis **Ephesus**

Corinth ★

B

MELITA

LY

CRETE RHO

Lasea ★ Salmone

M e d i t e r r a n e a n   S e a

Cyrene ★

CYRENAICA

Map 28

★ Rome

★ Puteoli

PAUL'S MISSION

Philippi ★

Beroea ★

★ Troy

Assos ★

Delphi ★

Antioch

★ Rhegium

Athens ★

Ephesus

Lystra ★ Derbe ★ Tarsus

Corinth ★

Attalia

Antioch

★ Syracuse

★ Salamis

Lasea ★ Salmone

Paphos

M e d i t e r r a n e a n   S e a

Damas

Tyre ★

Paul's first
missionary journey,
A.D.46–48.

Cyrene ★

Caesarea ★

Jerusalem

Paul's second
missionary journey,
A.D.49–52.

Paul's third
missionary journey,
A.D.53–57.

Alexandria ★

0   100   200

Paul's journey to Rome,
A.D.59–62.

0   100   200 km

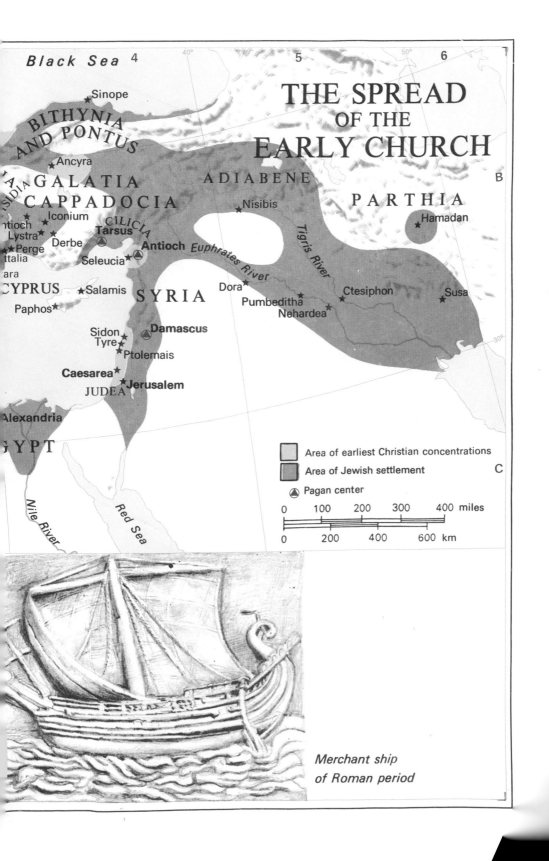

Black Sea

Sinope

BITHYNIA
AND PONTUS

Ancyra

GALATIA

CAPPADOCIA

ADIABENE

PARTHIA

Nisibis

Hamadan

Iconium

ntioch

CILICIA

Lystra

Tarsus

Derbe

Antioch

Euphrates River

ttalia

Perge

Seleucia

ara

Dora

CYPRUS

Salamis

SYRIA

Tigris River

Ctesiphon

Susa

Paphos

Pumbeditha

Nehardea

Sidon

Damascus

Tyre

Ptolemais

Caesarea

Jerusalem

JUDEA

Alexandria

GYPT

Nile River

Red Sea

THE SPREAD
OF THE
EARLY CHURCH

B

C

Area of earliest Christian concentrations

Area of Jewish settlement

Pagan center

0   100   200   300   400 miles

0   200   400   600 km

Merchant ship
of Roman period

THE GROWTH OF CHRISTIANITY

(29)

A

IX

VIII

Eburacum

Lindum

IV

VII

Londinium

VIII

Colonia Agrippina

Danube River

V

Lugdunum

Vienna

Arelate

Massilia

Salon

B

V

Rome

Corduba

Puteoli

256
Carthage

Syracuse

Medite

C

| | Extent of Christian church, A.D. 1st cent. | | Extent of Christian church, A.D. 2nd cent. | ⚚ Notable early church |

⊕ Major church council
431 (with date)

IV Century of conversion to Christianity

COPTS Monophysite church after 431

•••••••• Boundary of Roman Empire

||||||||| Split of Latin (western) and Greek (eastern) churches, A.D. 5th cent.

```
0        200       400       600 miles
0    200   400   600   800 km
```

carta

4   45°   5   60°   60°

A

45°

IX

IX

XI

Christian victims in the arena

Black Sea

B

Anchialus

Sinope

Amastris

Amisos

Adrianopolis

Melitene

Constantinople *381*

Chalcedon   Nicomedia

ARMENIANS

ilippi

Beroea

451   Nicaea

325

Samosata

opolis

Pergamum

JACOBITES

ne   Athens   Sardes

Tarsus

Edessa

Nisibis

Aegina

Ephesus

Antioch

431

Laodicea

Apamea

Dura
Europos

Tigris River

Knossos

Salamis

Euphrates River

Paphos

nean   Sea

Tyre

Cyrene

Caesarea

Jerusalem

49

Alexandria

COPTS

C

Mt. Sinai

Nile River

*Red
Sea*

3   30°   4   45°

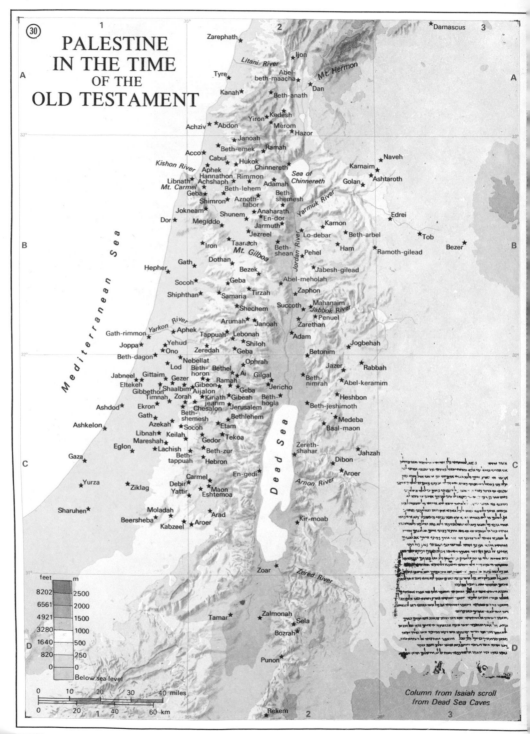

PALESTINE
IN THE TIME
OF THE
OLD TESTAMENT

Damascus

Zarephath

Litani River · Ijon

Tyre · Abel-beth-maacha · Mt. Hermon

Kanah · Dan

Beth-anath

Achziv · Abdon · Yiron · Kedesh · Merom · Hazor

Janoah

Acco · Beth-emek · Ramah

Cabul · Hukok · Naveh

Kishon River · Aphek · Chinnereth · Karnaim

Libnath · Hannathon · Rimmon · Sea of Chinnereth · Ashtaroth

Achshaph · Adamah · Golan

Mt. Carmel · Beth-lehem

Geba · Shimron · Aznoth-tabor · Beth-shemesh

Jokneam · Shunem · Anaharath · Kamon

Dor · Megiddo · En-dor · Edrei

Jezreel · Jarmuth · Lo-debar · Beth-arbel · Tob

Iron · Taanach · Beth-shean · Pehel · Ham · Ramoth-gilead · Bezer

Mt. Gilboa

Hepher · Gath · Dothan · Bezek · Jabesh-gilead

Socoh · Geba · Abel-meholah

Shiphthan · Samaria · Tirzah · Zaphon

Shechem · Succoth · Mahanaim · Jabbok River

Arumah · Janoah · Penuel

Gath-rimmon · Yarkon River · Aphek · Tappuah · Lebonah · Zarethan

Joppa · Yehud · Zeredah · Shiloh · Adam

Beth-dagon · Ono · Geba · Betonim

Nebellat · Ophrah

Lod · Beth-horon · Bethel · Jazer · Rabbah

Jabneel · Gittaim · Gezer · Ramah · Ai · Gilgal

Eltekeh · Shaalbim · Gibeon · Aijalon · Jericho · Beth-nimrah · Abel-keramim

Gibbethon · Timnah · Zorah · Kiriath-jearim · Gibeah · Beth-hogla · Heshbon

Ashdod · Ekron · Chesalon · Jerusalem

Gath · Beth-shemesh · Bethlehem · Beth-jeshimoth

Ashkelon · Azekah · Socoh · Etam · Medeba

Libnah · Keilah · Baal-maon

Mareshah · Gedor · Tekoa · Zereth-shahar

Gaza · Eglon · Lachish · Beth-zur · Jahzah

Beth-tappuah · Hebron · Dibon · Aroer

Carmel · En-gedi

Yurza · Ziklag · Debir · Maon · Arnon River

Yattir · Eshtemoa

Sharuhen · Moladah · Arad

Beersheba · Kabzeel · Aroer · Kir-moab

Zoar · Zered River

Mediterranean Sea

Jordan River

Yarmuk River

Dead Sea

Tamar · Zalmonah · Sela

Bozrah

Punon

Rekem

feet	m
8202	2500
6561	2000
4921	1500
3280	1000
1640	500
820	250
0	0
	Below sea level

0   10   20   30   40 miles

0   20   40   60 km

*Column from Isaiah scroll
from Dead Sea Caves*

carta

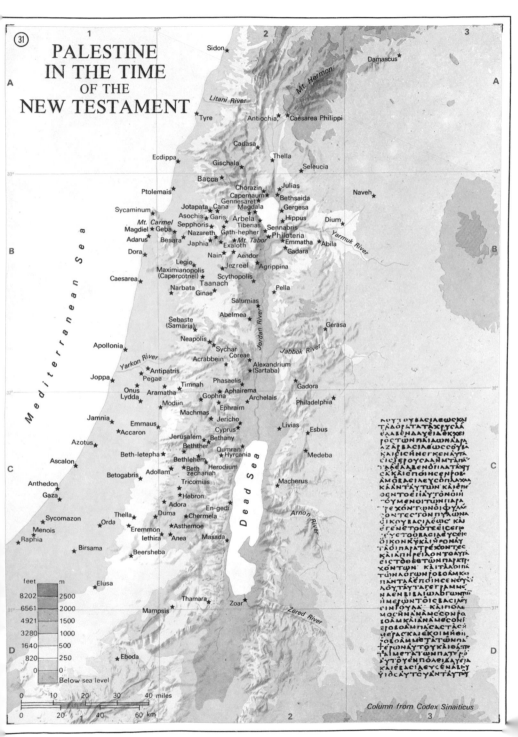

PALESTINE IN THE TIME OF THE NEW TESTAMENT

Column from Codex Sinaiticus

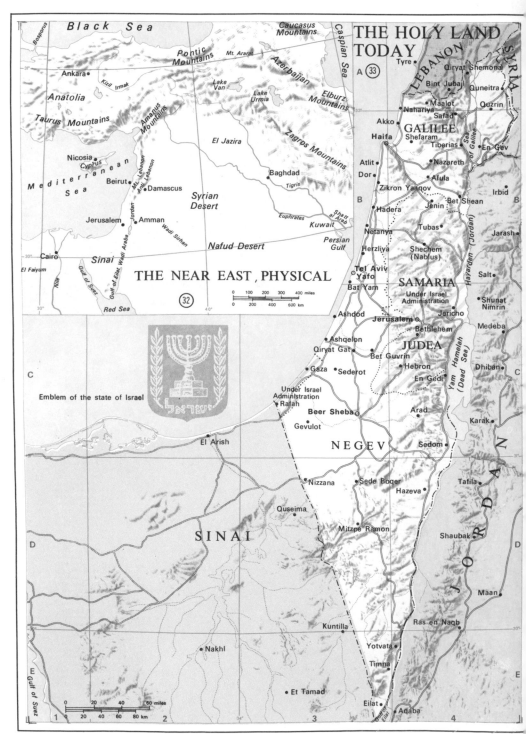

THE HOLY LAND TODAY

A ㉝

THE NEAR EAST, PHYSICAL

㉜

| 0 | 100 | 200 | 300 | 400 miles |
| 0 | 200 | 400 | 600 km |

Black Sea

Caucasus Mountains

Pontic Mountains   Mt. Ararat

Caspian Sea

Ankara   Kızıl Irmak

Azerbaijan

Lake Van

Lake Urmia

Elburz Mountains

Anatolia

Taurus Mountains

Amanus Mountains

El Jazira

Zagros Mountains

Nicosia

Cyprus

Mediterranean Sea

Beirut

Anti-Lebanon
Mt. Lebanon

Damascus

Baghdad

Tigris

Syrian Desert

Euphrates

Shatt al Arab

Kuwait

Jerusalem   Jordan   Amman

Wadi Sirhan

Persian Gulf

Cairo

Sinai

Nafud Desert

El Faiyum

Nile

Gulf of Suez

Gulf of Eilat, Wadi Araba

Red Sea

Emblem of the state of Israel

Tyre

Qiryat Shemona

Bint Jubail

Quneitra

Maalot

Qazrin

Nahariya   Safad

Akko   GALILEE   Shefaram

Haifa   Tiberias   En Gev

Sea of Galilee

Atlit   Nazareth

Dor   Afula

Zikron Yaaqov   Irbid

Bet Shean

Hadera   Jenin

Netanya   Tubas   Jarash

Herzliya   Shechem (Nablus)

Tel Aviv   Salt

Yafo   SAMARIA

Bat Yam   Under Israel Administration   Shunat Nimrin

Ashdod   Jerusalem   Jericho

Bethlehem   Medeba

Ashqelon   JUDEA   Dhiban

Qiryat Gat   Bet Guvrin   Hebron

Gaza   Sederot   En Gedi   Karak

Under Israel Administration   Rafah

Beer Sheba   Arad

Gevulot   Sedom

NEGEV

El Arish

Nizzana   Sede Boqer   Tafila

Quseima   Hazeva

Mitzpe Ramon   Shaubak

SINAI   JORDAN

Maan

Kuntilla   Ras en Naqb

Nakhl   Yotvata

Timna

Et Tamad   Eilat   Aqaba

| 0 | 20 | 40 | 60 miles |
| 0 | 20 | 40 | 60 | 80 km |

© carta